Shane Stanley's
Noosa Farmers' Market

Petra Frieser

pebbles in the sky

Dedicated to the wonderful growers and producers of the Sunshine Coast for allowing us all to enjoy fresh, quality food.

Shane Stanley's Noosa Farmers' Market
by Petra Frieser

Designed by Pebbles in the Sky
Photography by Petra Frieser and Maggie Ensor

Published by Pebbles in the Sky 2007

Pebbles in the Sky
PO Box 1975
Sunshine Plaza, Qld 4558
www.pebblesinthesky.com.au
info@pebblesinthesky.com.au

© 2007 Text Petra Frieser
© 2007 Images Petra Frieser
© 2007 Images Maggie Ensor, Pages 8, 9, 24 & 25

Printed in Australia by Fergies Print & Mail, Brisbane, Australia

The National Library of Australia Cataloguing-in-Publication Data:
Frieser, Petra
  Shane Stanley's Noosa Farmers' Market / author, Petra
          Frieser; photographer, Petra Frieser.
1st Edition
Publisher: Maroochydore, Qld. : Pebbles in the Sky, 2007.
ISBN: 9780980306811 (pbk.) :

Noosa Farmer's Market (Noosaville, Qld.)
Farmer's markets--Queensland--Noosaville.
Recipes.
381.41099432

All rights reserved. No part of this publication may be reproduced, stored in a retrieval system, or transmitted in any form by any means, electronic, mechanical, photocopying, recording or otherwise without prior permission of the publishers and copyright holders.

This book is a Regional Foodie initiative
www.regionalfoodie.com.au

Table of Contents

Introduction   5

Spring 11

      Marinated Goat's Curd with Pickled Baby Beets 12
      Chermoula Marinated Cuttlefish with Yoghurt Sauce . . 15
      Spicy Croc Bites 16

Summer 19

      Spanner Crab Brandade on Grilled Sourdough 20
      Raincherry and Peach Summer Pudding 23

Autumn 27

      Friands 28
      Tempura Vegetables 30
      Pommes Banskia 33

Winter 35

      Noosa Farmers' Market Pizzas 36
      Bushfood Ravioli 39
      Sticky Lamb Shanks with Parsnip Mash 40

Noosa Farmers' Market Directory 42

Acknowledgements 46

Introduction

Growing up on a farm, I have always sung the virtues of fresh regionally produced food. Experiencing fruit fresh from the tree or vegies straight from the garden is a delight like no other. It appeases a kaleidoscope of senses, through its fragrance, its clarity of flavour and texture and once the delight has been discovered seeking out the freshest and the best becomes a way of life.

The Sunshine Coast is blessed in so many ways when it comes to fresh produce, the climate fitting to so many growing applications; tropical fruits throughout the seasons; vegetables, green and crisp; native foods, a new innovative industry; the list goes on. There are the artisan cheeses that are sold by the cheese makers themselves alongside freshly baked home-style sour dough and wholegrain breads, cakes and slices. Then of course there is the wonderful assortment of condiments in the way of exquisite fruity jams, savoury pestos and pickles, olives, tapenades, luscious olive oils, handmade meze and antipasto selections produced by dedicated producers who go one step further in the production process by plying base products into something much more magnificent. There are farmers who breed livestock with integrity and humanity and fisherman with seafood as well as other great industry innovators who go out on a limb to do something unique and thereby educating a whole new realm of gourmands keen to explore the merits of a prize yet unknown.

Noosa has always been a great supporter and innovator of these industries. Chefs have long sung their praises also, spectacularly accenting their meals and menus with ingredients that are individually named, as if by naming the producer or region from which it has come, it defines not just what it is but also the quality and freshness of which the diner will be assured. The wonderful thing is that through the advent of farmers' markets that have sprouted in most of the major growing regions, that same fresh quality produce is now available to us all.

The Noosa Farmers' Market is one of the most well known and frequented markets on the Sunshine Coast. Every week stall holders set up shop in the early hours of the morning while most of us are still asleep. With them they bring fruits and vegetables, freshly harvested, breads still warm from the oven and other

wonderful produce that spills from beneath a canopy of marquees like vibrant precious jewels.

Shane Stanley and his lovely partner, Lisa are the people behind the Noosa Farmers' Markets, the idea sparked in 2001 when an associate approached Shane with the dream of creating a commercial opportunity for local farmers and producers through way of a market. Shane had always loved the idea of buying straight from the producer and when the opportunity presented itself he knew there was a big future for the farmers' market in Noosa as the number of high quality producers scattered throughout the hinterland was unique in itself.

The Noosa Farmers' Market saw its first trading day on Sunday 24th November 2002, with 28 stall holders and around 500 customers. Held monthly, by the third market, stall holders had risen to 60 and the markets had close to 3,000 customers, a huge jump from the previous two markets. That's when Shane knew that they had created something special. The feedback on the fresh produce was the best advertising the market could have had; it wasn't long before people flocked to the market and they have done so ever since.

Inevitably the market quickly outgrew one trading day per month and the decision was made to trade fortnightly in June 2003. The market again seemed to go from strength to strength. It became a focus point for many activities such as the Noosa Food & Wine Trail and had kick-started a huge awareness of local producers and foods. When the market had reached its capacity 3 years sooner than anticipated, the options were to move to a bigger venue or trade weekly. A joint decision was reached between Shane and the producers to trade weekly from December 2006, meaning the markets could retain its small village appeal and appease the farmers that were calling for weekly trading.

Shane kept the activity exclusively for farmers and producers and chose to exclude local arts and crafts

people who he believed had many more selling opportunities than producers and he retained the fundamental principle of the markets; that the markets were not a market for market sake, but a real commercial option for local producers to create an income.

The next 5 years of the market's journey looks to be very exciting as it gains national recognition and Shane personally takes pride in what the producers and he have created in such a short time. Shane's goal when they started the Noosa Farmers' Market was to develop a farmers' market in every region on the Sunshine and Cooloola Coasts supporting local growers and to create an activity where producers could meet consumers and pass on their stories and challenges. September 1st 2007 saw the beginning of the Big Pineapple Farmers' Market which so far has been equally successful, fulfilling the wish list of many foodies south of Noosa. The awareness of local produce increases, not just due to the markets efforts, but also due to the people who have taken the challenge to promote local Australian Food.

The beauty of the Noosa Farmers' Market and farmers markets' in general is the interaction with the stall holders and their eagerness to share tips and stories, recipes and ideas on how to use their products or what's in season at that point in time. They become almost like friends with weekly morning exchanges of banter and bounty. To add to it all, are gorgeous cut flowers and plants, local musicians, freshly brewed coffee, juices or a wheatgrass shot as well as a selection of savoury and sweet snacks and meals to complete an entertaining morning market experience, one that we will hopefully continue to experience for many years to come.

The following pages are a celebration of the food, the markets and the camaraderie of a community that sees the intrinsic value of supporting their local industries and the reward by way of quality, fresh and above all, regionally produced food.

Enjoy!

Spring

For many, spring marks the beginning of the seasonal calendar and although Queensland is blessed with a climate that sees many, otherwise seasonal fruit and vegetables grown throughout the year, spring always brings with it that additional selection of edible treats.

Fresh tender asparagus spears, vibrant leafy greens and aromatic herbs line the stalls with the onset of this magical season. Strawberries lush and fragrant delight market-goers as they find it hard to pass the punnets bursting with fruit. Sun ripened tomatoes, sweet corn in their husks, recently unearthed potatoes and fresh goat's curd, all part of a vigorous new season's bounty.

Spring means ...
Eating fresh **strawberries**, dusted with icing sugar or taking home the 'seconds' to make your own jam... filling **zucchini flowers** with **gorgonzola** or creamy **fetta** and deep frying in batter... pickling baby **beetroot** to be served with marinated **goat's curd** and **lavosh** or baked in foil and then drizzled with **olive oil** and **chives**... new season **potatoes**, steamed and sprinkled with **macadamia oil** and **wattleseed** or **purple congos** fried into wafer-thin chips... a mélange of baby **rocket**, **oakleaf**, **buttercrunch** and **cos lettuce** drizzled with a fruity chilli and lime extra virgin **olive oil** scattered with fresh **herbs**... fragrant sun-ripened **tomatoes** served with fresh crusty **sourdough** and a **spanner crab** brandade or **cherry tomatoes** in their clusters slow roasted and sprinkled with balsamic vinegar... **sugarsnap peas**, **snowpeas** and **peas** prised from their pods served soused with nut brown **butter** and **mint**...

Look out for...
Noosa Valley Market Garden's leafy greens, beetroot and Asian vegetables; **Bedrock Herb's** baby spinach and leafy greens; **Hinterland Organic's** fresh seasonal fruit and vegetables throughout the year; **Eumundi Strawberries, Kandara Strawberries** and **Sunray Berries'** fresh flavoursome strawberries; **Waugh's Fruit & Vegetables'** fresh seasonal fruit and vegetables; **Gympie Cheese's** fresh goat's curd and handmade butter; **Gabbana's Fruit & Vegetables'** fresh seasonal vegetables; **Crystal Waters Bakery's** fresh crusty sourdough breads; **Kenilworth Organic Olive Oil's** extra virgin olive oils; **Dev's Herbs'** fresh herbs and leafy greens and **Newman's Asparagus**, delicious tender asparagus and selected herbs ... **Ray Atkin's** and **Noosa Reds'** luscious fragrant vine ripened tomatoes... Tayaki's tasty Japanese pancakes.

Marinated Goat's Curd with Pickled Baby Beets

Recipe by Matt Golinski, The Rolling Dolmade

This makes a lovely light lunch dish or entrée. You can also cheat by buying ready made pickled baby beets (The Rolling Dolmade) at the markets. A variety of Lavosh and artisan breads are also available there; grilled sourdough bread makes a great alternative to the Lavosh.

Ingredients:

For the Curd:
1 round fresh goat's curd (approx 250g)
1/2 cup extra virgin olive oil
A few sprigs of fresh thyme
1/4 tsp roasted fennel seeds
2 cloves garlic, crushed
8 black peppercorns

For the Beets:
24 baby beets, ends trimmed
1 cup red wine vinegar
1 cup water
1/3 cup sugar
1 tsp salt
6 bay leaves
1/2 tsp coriander seeds
1/2 tsp black peppercorns

6 sheets of lavosh to serve
Cress to serve

Method:

Prepare the curd by cutting the curd into 6 equal rounds and lay flat in a dish. Mix together the rest of the ingredients and pour over the curd. Refrigerate until ready to use. This is best done 2-3 days before serving.

Boil the beets in salted water until the skins rub off easily. Cool & peel. Boil together the rest of the ingredients and simmer for five minutes. Pack the beets into a sterilized glass jar and pour pickling liquid over.

To serve, place a round of curd and four beets on each plate. Roughly crack the Lavosh and stack 4-5 pieces on each plate. Garnish with cress and some of the marinating oil.

Serves 6

Chermoula Marinated Cuttlefish with Yoghurt Sauce

Recipe by Matt Golinski, The Rolling Dolmade

The fresh, zesty flavours of this marinade lends itself well to all seafood, but especially compliments cuttlefish.

Ingredients:

500gm cuttlefish
1 garlic clove
1 tbs ginger
1 bunch coriander
1 red chilli
1 small red onion
zest of 1 lemon
1 tsp ground cumin
1 tsp ground coriander
100ml olive oil
250ml greek yoghurt
1/2 continental cucumber, finely grated
1/4 cup mint, finely chopped
salt & pepper
24 wooden skewers

Method:

Clean and score the cuttlefish and cut into small triangles. Put garlic, ginger, coriander, chilli, onion, zest and spices into a food processor and blend to a paste, adding oil to help it blend. Mix with cuttlefish and place 3 pieces of cuttlefish on each skewer. Season with salt and pepper. Cook skewers on barbeque until golden, about 2 minutes on each side.

Whisk together yoghurt, cucumber and mint. Season with salt and pepper.

Serve cuttlefish immediately drizzled with the sauce or with sauce in a dish on the side.

Serves 4

Spicy Croc Bites

Recipe by Peter Wolfe, Cedar Creek Farm

These spicy rolls are delicious way of utilising crocodile meat however any meat can be used if crocodile meat is unavailable to you. Crocodile meat is a lean white meat, and available from the Noosa Farmers' Market, so look out for it. The markets also sell a wonderful range of dipping sauces and condiments that could accompany the rolls.

Ingredients:

2 tbs macadamia oil
15g fresh ginger
15g fresh galangal
15g fresh turmeric
15g fresh garlic
1 small onion
30g macadamia nuts
1 tsp each of paprika, chilli powder, cumin and pepper
1 cup coconut milk
1 cup water
250g crocodile meat
300g mixed finely sliced vegetables such as cabbage, carrot, onion, green beans, bean sprouts
24 spring roll skins
Salt to taste
Soy sauce to taste
Macadamia oil for frying

Method:

Finely blend or grind in a mortar; macadamia oil, ginger, galangal, turmeric, garlic, onion and macadamia nuts. Cook over a low flame until aromatic then add spices. Cook for a few more minutes until you have a thick paste then add coconut cream and water. Reduce until you have a thick sauce and season with soy, salt and more chilli if you prefer spicy food. Finely slice the crocodile and place in the sauce to cook. Sauté the vegetables in a separate pan then add to the sauce and crocodile mix. Heat together for two minutes then take off the stove and place the mixture in the refrigerator to cool. The mixture should be coated with the sauce not soggy and sitting in a puddle of it.

When the mixture has cooled separate your spring roll skins. Place the same amount of filling in each and roll into a neat cylinder. Seal the ends with a little paste of flour and water. Allow to rest for one hour then fry until golden brown in macadamia oil. Serve immediately with soy or chilli dipping sauce.

Makes approximately 24 spring rolls.

Summer

For the Queensland tropics summer is a contradictive balance of sweltering heat and tropical deluges that rally the crops through a peak growing season. Tropical fruits are bountiful; scented fruits such as lychees, mangos, figs and beautiful juicy peaches, a whole spectrum of delectable berries, melons and bananas, grow lush and abundantly on the coast and have come to be synonymous with the tropics. Christmas feasts are sumptuously embellished with fresh garden salads, seafood fresh from the trawlers and fishermen and baskets bursting with a constellation of freshly selected fruits. Summer itself makes way for all things refreshing; sorbets and ices, smoothies and sodas...

Summer means ...
Sorbets made from the pearly white flesh of the **lychee** or the juicy sweet fruit of the **mango**... torn **figs** laced with fresh **goat's fetta** and drizzled with organic **olive oil** and cracked pepper... the **spanner crab's** delicate flesh handpicked and enjoyed with a glass of white **wine**... antipasto platters mounded with pickled **pimentos de padrone**, **eggplant** and **quinces**, marinated **olives** and an assortment of herby **pestos** and **tapenades**... fragrant summer **berries** doused with liqueurs and homemade **yoghurt**... roast free-range **pork** lavished with **raincherry** sauce... tea smoked **salmon** served on **hommus** and sprinkled with **rocket pesto** and roasted **macadamia nuts**... fresh **mango** salsa spiked with blazing hot **chilli**... moist Christmas **puddings** with fresh double **cream**... wok-fried **bok choy** and **oyster mushrooms** drizzled with **kaffir lime oil** and **coriander** shreds...free range farm **egg** frittata with **zucchini** and **swiss chard**.

Look out for...
Spanners Crabs Noosa's live spanner crabs and locally caught seafood; **Alison & Peter King's** fresh strawberries and avocados; **The Eumundi Food Company's** Christmas pudding and friands; **Crystal Waters Wood Fired Bakery's** cherry and chocolate sourdough bread; **Slow Rise Bakery's** biscotti and cakes; **The Rolling Dolmade's** piquillo peppers stuffed with **Coolabine Farmstead** goat's cheese; **Wheatgrass Noosa's** wheatgrass shots, **The Mango Shack's** mango smoothies and ices; **Claude's Salads**, roast pumpkin, spinach and Thai coconut dressing salad; **Liz's Own Antipasto's** marinated mushrooms and olives; **Wort Organic's** lemon and ginger organic soft drink; **Galeru's** rainberry and raincherry condiments and cakes; **Fat Hen Farm's** flavoured olive oils and tapenades; **Back Pocket's** pickpocket rosé.

Spanner Crab Brandade on Grilled Sourdough

Recipe by Matt Golinski, The Rolling Dolmade

This is a superb way of utilising fresh crab meat and makes for a delicious summer lunch. Spanner Crabs Noosa sells live spanner crabs at the Noosa Farmers' Market every week. There are also a fabulous assortment of sourdough breads available at the markets baked fresh by local artisan bakers.

Ingredients:

200g potatoes, peeled and diced (preferably Sebago or Desiree)
250g spanner crab meat, fresh
1 clove garlic, crushed
1tbs chopped flat parsley
salt & pepper

For the Salad:

100ml extra virgin olive oil
1 punnet cherry tomatoes
1 punnet yellow cherry tomatoes
4 small vine-ripened tomatoes
1 small red onion, fine rings
½ cup basil leaves, picked & torn
¼ cup red wine vinegar
¼ cup extra virgin olive oil

1 loaf crusty sourdough, cut into six 2.5cm slices
1 clove garlic, extra
extra virgin olive oil, extra

Method:

Boil the potatoes in salted water until soft, drain and pass through a mouli or ricer, or mash until smooth. Cool.
Add crab, garlic, parsley, salt and pepper and work with fork into a rough paste. Slowly drizzle in the olive oil, working gently to emulsify without loosing the texture of the crab. Check seasoning and refrigerate.

Halve cherry tomatoes and cut vine-ripened tomatoes into wedges. Mix with onion rings & basil and set aside. Brush sourdough with oils and grill until crispy on both sides. Rub each piece with a cut garlic clove. Spread each bruschetta (the grilled bread) with a generous amount of brandade and put on a plate. Dress the tomato salad with oil and vinegar, season and arrange on top of brandade. Drizzle with extra oil and serve immediately.

Serves 6

Note:

To make this recipe you will need to cook the Spanner Crab as per the instructions given to you by the supplier or visit Spanner Crabs Noosa's profile on my Local Harvest website:
www.localharvest.com.au/content/view/126

Raincherry & Peach Summer Pudding

Recipe by Brent Southcombe, Designed 2 Taste

This is a decadent combination of summer berries, topped with Raincherries. Raincherries are the fruit of an Australian native Syzygium fibrosum and are grown and preserved locally by Galeru. They have an almost cinnamon x plum flavoured fruit that is quite unique, and the perfect compliment to these other summer fruits. Although the buttery flavour of the brioche is perfect for this recipe, a light sweet spelt dough would work well also.

Ingredients:

Sugar Syrup:
250g castor sugar
250ml water
Juice of half a lemon

Blackberry Coulis:
250g frozen blackberries
6 tbs sugar syrup (above)

2 peaches, cut in half
2 tsp demerara sugar
8 (1cm thick) slices of brioche
125g strawberries, hulled
½ cup of blueberries
½ punnet of raspberries
8 tbs raincherries

Method:

Place sugar, water and lemon juice in a pot and bring to a simmer. Remove and allow to cool; store excess in an airtight container in the fridge to use another time. Simmer blackberries and sugar syrup in a pot until blackberries break down, then puree in a food processor and rub through a fine sieve. Pre-heat oven to 180°C and roast the peaches by cutting them in half and coating them with Demerara sugar. This should take about 25 minutes.

Using a 5-6 centimetre round cookie cutter, cut 12 circles out of the brioche slices. Dip the brioche circles in the blackberry coulis coating both sides. Place four round cookie cutters on a serving dish each and using them as a mould, place a disk of brioche at the bottom of each cutter, to make the first layer. Next, layer with sliced strawberries then put a spoon of coulis over the top, followed by another slice of blackberry coulis coated brioche. Place blueberries on the next level, topped with another slice of coated brioche and finally place raspberries on the top in a circle.

To finish pudding, lift the mould (the cookie cutter) to expose the beautiful layers. Top the stack with a roasted peach half each and spoon over Raincherries with a little of their own syrup. Serve Immediately.

Serves 4

Autumn

Autumn months on the coast are a gentle wind down from summer. Days are milder and late harvests become the essence of winter provisions in the way of preserves and condiments. Fruits are in abundance, apples, pears and quinces, some grown locally, others from a little more south.

Olives are harvested and cold pressed for the first drops of extra virgin olive oil granting the fruity heart of so many recipes, dressings and marinades. Greens that may have struggled through summer now grow with revived vigour; swiss chard, silverbeet, fennel and Warrigul greens. Soul food begins to creep into our thoughts as we see the appearance of pumpkins and root vegetables and we almost look forward to the promise of some cooler nights and earthy harvests.

Autumn means ...
Delicious poached **quinces** with a dollop of **rainberry yoghurt**... crates of **apples**, fresh and crisp, delicately poached with **cinnamon** and **star anise**... baked **quark** cheesecake served warm subtly scented with the zest of dew kissed **citrus** fruits... steamed **cauliflower** and **broccoli** sprinkled with **gorgonzola dolce** and toasted **almond** flakes ... **snapper** baked on a bed of baby **fennel** drizzled with **lemon myrtle** infused extra virgin **olive oil**... an earthy **mushroom** and **duck** risotto made divine with scatterings of **preserved lemon** and butter browned **sage**... boiled **sapphire potatoes** lavishly coated with **wasabi mayonnaise** served steaming... freshly baked **rye** generously topped with **lillypilly and lychee jam**... poached free range **eggs** with buttered **swiss chard** and gratings of **tilsit cheese**.

Look out for...
Maleny Cheese's buffalo brie and gorgonzola dolce; **Hollaran's Fruit**, new season apples and pears; **Spunky Spuds'** sapphire and purple potatoes; **Sue's Organic Cuisine's** rosella jam and flavoured mayonnaise and aioli; **Villarica's** juicy passionfruit; **Fromart's** tilsit cheese and fresh quark; **Natural Greek Yoghurt's** strawberry and mango yoghurt; **Essential Grain Bakery's** freshly baked panini; **Eco Australia**, locally grown, honey-coated macadamia nuts; **Exotic Mushrooms'** shiitake, enoki and oyster mushrooms; **Farmer Bill's** fresh herbs and lettuce; **Cedar Creek Farm's** mountain pepperberry jam... **North Shore Gourmet's** tasty dips and homemade jams... **Soul Food's** New Orlean's style sauces... **Stockman's Choice Meats**, Queensland gourmet beef as well as crocodile and kangaroo meat.

Friands

Recipe by Mary Bowtle, The Eumundi Food Company

Friands (also known in Paris as 'financiers') are small cakes, traditionally made with almond meal, topped with fruit and dusted with icing sugar. A Sunshine Coast twist on this recipe calls for ground Australian native macadamia nuts instead of almond meal.

Ingredients:
150g butter
100g ground macadamias
5 large egg whites
210g pure icing sugar
160g self raising flour
Seasonal fruit such as berries, raincherries, lychees, pineapples, passionfruit, marmalade, crystallised ginger etc.

Method:
Grease a non-stick friand or muffin baking tray with butter and sprinkle with cornflour. Preheat oven to 150°C. Melt butter. Mix all dry ingredients together and then stir in lightly beaten egg whites. Stir in the melted butter ensuring not to over beat.

Top friands with local fruit in season or fold the zest of 2 lemons or 2 limes through the mix.

To ensure the fruit stays on the top of the friand, freeze the fruit first, otherwise it will sink. Slice or dice large fruits. Bake at 150°C for 25 minutes.

Serve friands at room temperature for afternoon tea or warm with a custard made from the egg yolks for dessert.

Makes 12

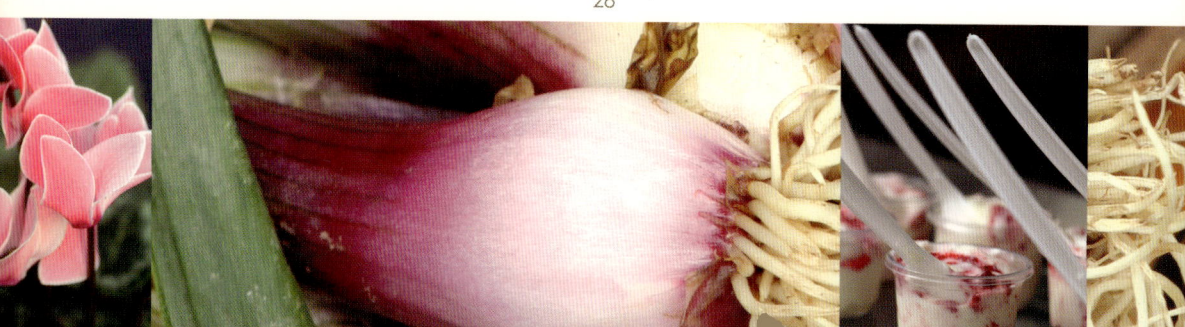

Tempura Vegetables

Recipe by Local Harvest

The market has some wonderful fresh fruit and vegetables throughout the seasons. A delicious and easy vegetable snack is to batter and deep fry chunky slices. Any combination of vegetables can be used, be it eggplant, enoki mushrooms, brocolini or cheese filled zucchini flowers. The trick to a good tempura batter is for it to be icy cold and lumpy, just a quick whisk is fine and once deep fried serve immediately so it is nice and crisp. Serve with a chilli or soy dipping sauce. Prawns are fabulous cooked in this way also.

Ingredients:
50g cornflour
50g self-raising flour
2 tbs olive oil
200ml soda water – icy cold
peanut oil for deep frying

Choose from:
eggplant wedges
mushrooms – exotic or Swiss browns
brocolini, peas & okra
capsicum
sweet potato
sapphire potatoes
baby carrots
bok choy

Try also:
zucchini flowers stuffed with
gorgonzola dolce or goat's fetta
fresh fruit slices
prawns, oysters or scallops

Method:
Select an assortment of vegetables allowing 3-4 pieces for each person depending on size. Prepare and slice all the vegetables or other ingredients to be used and set aside ready for frying. Place cornflour and self-raising flour in a mixing bowl. Add macadamia nut oil and soda water to the flours and give a very quick whisk leaving plenty of lumps and flour clinging to the bowl. Heat the frying oil to approximately 190 °C. One by one roughly coat vegetables with lumpy tempura mix and lower into oil. Fry vegetables in small batches removing each one as it turns golden. Serve immediately.

If deep frying stuffed zucchini flowers, gently fill each flower with a teaspoon of cheese. Gorgonzola dolce is particularly good as is the fetta and brie. Be careful when coating the flowers with batter as they are quite delicate and can easily snap off. Chillis can also be cooked in this way, but are not for the faint hearted!!

Pommes Banskia

Recipe by Peter Wolfe, Cedar Creek Farm

I have been fascinated with purple and blue potatoes ever since I first discovered them at the Noosa Farmers' Market. The flesh of this vegetable is a vibrant purple or blue when sliced in half and is quite spectacular. It can loose a little of its vibrancy in the cooking process so boiling them with their skins on is the best way to retain their colour. The mash may also be flavoured with fresh herbs, garlic or onion.

Ingredients:

250g purple congo or sapphire potatoes
300g white potatoes
175ml beer
250g self-raising flour
3 tbs cream
3 tbs butter
salt and pepper to taste
flour for dusting
oil for frying

Method:

Boil congo potatoes gently in the skin until tender. Drain and allow to cool slightly and then rub the skins off. Mash congo potatoes, season with salt and pepper and moisten with the cream and butter.

Peel the white potatoes and cut into matchstick sized pieces approximately 3-4cm long with a knife, mandolin or food processor. Mix together beer and flour and set aside.

Place the purple mash in a piping bag and pipe out one large log approximately 2 cm in diameter and then cut log into 5cm lengths. Dust these portions with flour then dip in batter. Remove from batter and roll in julienne potato strips until thinly but evenly coated. Fry in oil at 180°C until golden brown and crisp.

Makes approximately 12.

Winter

For the Sunshine Coast winter means cloudless blue skies and crisp wintry breezes and while it is nowhere near as cold as the southern states, it is still cold to us. The market shrouds itself in a layer of chilly mist in the early hours of the morning, the warm breath of the sun slowly warming the earth as the day progresses. This is where the market experience comes to the fore, brilliant winter spoils; beetroot, parsnips, pumpkin amongst the aroma of freshly brewed coffee, sizzling sausages and eggs and other fragrant delectables that waft to our noses from the stalls.

We yearn for comfort foods and soothe ourselves with steaming soups and slowly braised stews, yet there is also such an assortment of fresh produce available throughout these winter months. Giant garlic, onions and leeks make picturesque bunches while the spectacularly vivid blood oranges and persimmons appease the curious. Custard apples and pineapples pay homage to the tropics to the cycle of the seasons ready to begin all over again.

Winter means ...
The **blood oranges** red trimmed edges featuring brightly in winter salads... roasted **giant garlic** lathered onto grilled **sourdough bread**... creamy **potato** and **leek** soup dappled with **goat cheese** crumbs... slow braised **kangaroo** tail served with a **parsnip** and **brie** mash... grilled **pineapples** soused with rum and fresh dairy **cream**... bread and butter pudding made with farm fresh **eggs** and **wood fired bread**... **beetroot** tzatziki with a swirl of **garlic infused olive oil**... crisp flagrant **persimmons** sliced in a salad with **radicchio**, **walnuts** and **fetta**... **squid ink pasta** with seared **scallops** and fresh **herbs**... steaming hot **curry** served with a **banana**, **pineapple** and **mango chutney**.

Look out for...
Auswana Coffee's locally grown coffee; **Chimichurri Co's** piquant el chimichurri de papa traditional Argentinean sauce; **Brett Blackensee's** fresh pumpkin, broccoli and cauliflower; **Café Le Mundi's** pancakes; **Bean & Gone Coffee Cart's** freshly brewed coffee; **Cedar Creek Farm's** blood oranges and native pepperberry pasta; **Materia's** custard apples; **Mudgeeraba Spices'** spice blends, chutney's and take home meals; **North Shore Gourmet's** dips and chutneys; **Pasta Riviera's** pumpkin and basil fettuccine; **Supernatural Organic's** giant organic garlic; **Wensley's** Cornish pasties; **Hermitage Country Craft's** free range eggs and cakes and preserves; **Farmer Dave's** organic lamb.

Noosa Farmers' Market Pizzas

Recipe by Peter Wolfe, Cedar Creek Farm

The farmers' market is the perfect opportunity to be experimental with exciting pizza toppings and interesting combinations. There are dozens of condiments that can be spread on the sourdough base that sets the theme for the rest of the pizza; tomato relishes for a more traditional Italian style, curry pastes for a Indian themed or Asian style and pestos or tapenades for a tasty base to a vegetarian style. There is also no shortage of cheeses to choose as toppings; fetta, brie, camembert, Swiss style cheeses, goat's cheeses, gorgonzola, the list goes on. Here are 3 combinations to get you started but be adventurous and create your own as the combinations are truly endless.

Ingredients:

1 sourdough pizza base
Hommus
Salmon
Caperberries, fennel & exotic mushroom combinations
Macadamia nuts
Brie

or;

Pesto
Eggplant, capsicum & sweet potato
Fetta
Rocket

or;

Tomato pasta sauce or relish
Mixed olives
Semi dried tomatoes
Marinated mushrooms
Appenzeller or gruyere cheese

Method:

Spread hommus liberally onto the pizza base. Scatter with salmon, sliced into fine strips. Slice fennel lengthwise and barbequed on each side. Scatter fennel slices onto the base along with the caperberries, exotic mushrooms – enoki, shiitake and oyster, and macadamia nuts. Lay brie slices on top and bake at 220°C for approximately 10 minutes or until cheese is melted and nuts are golden brown.

or;
Spread pesto onto pizza base. Slice eggplant and sweet potato lengthwise and capsicum into quarters and barbeque on each side for a few minutes. Roughly shred barbequed vegetable slices and scatter over pizza base. Crumble fetta over the top. Bake for approximately 10 minutes at 220°C. Scatter rocket on top of baked pizza, drizzle with olive oil and serve.

or;
Spread tomato pasta sauce or relish over the pizza base. Scatter base with mixed olives, semi dried tomatoes and marinated mushrooms. Grate appenzeller or gruyere cheese and sprinkle over toppings. Bake for approximately 10 minutes at 220°C.

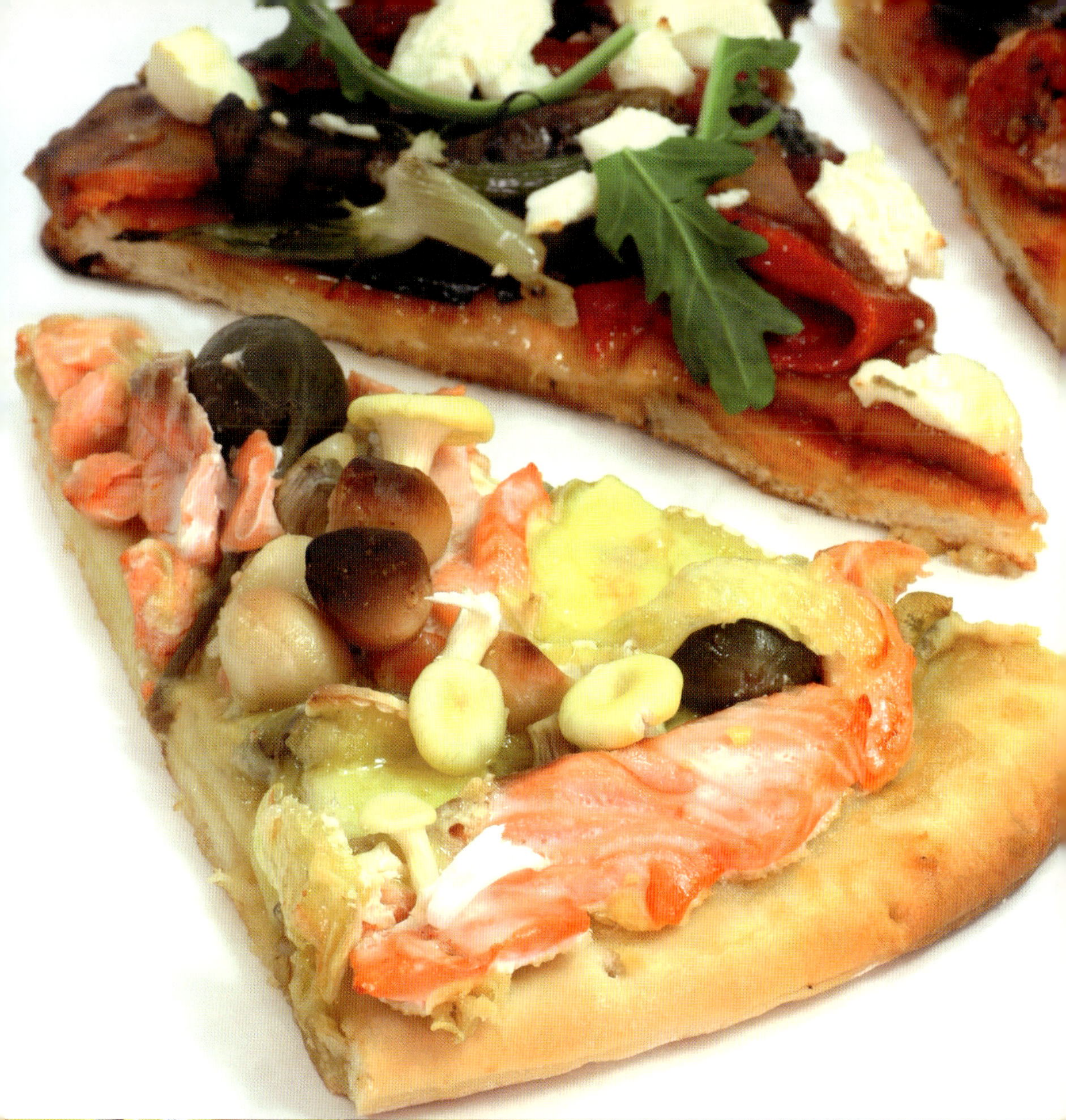

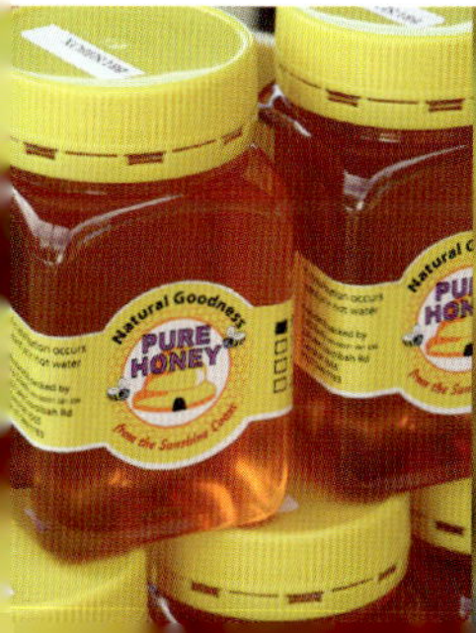
Natural Goodness
PURE HONEY

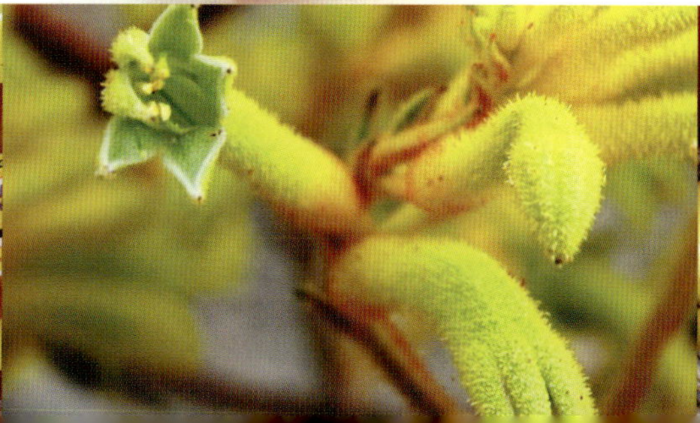

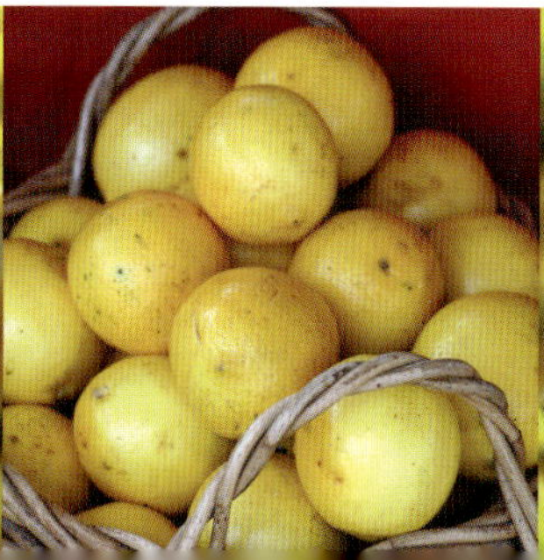

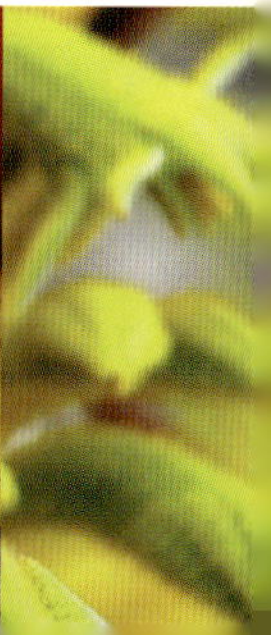

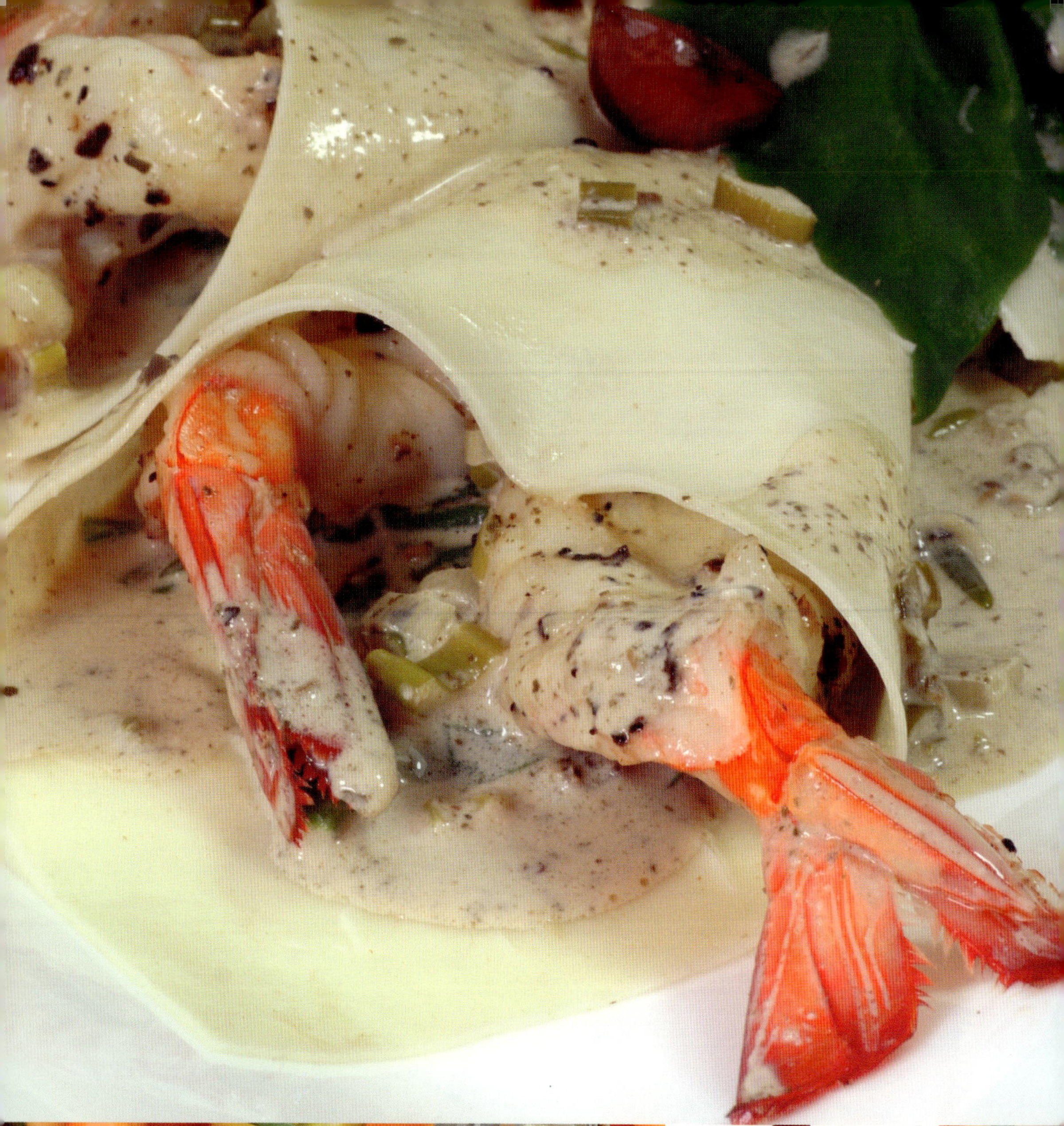

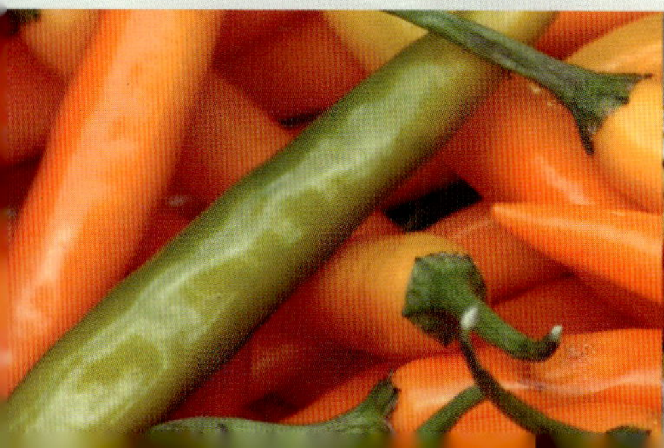

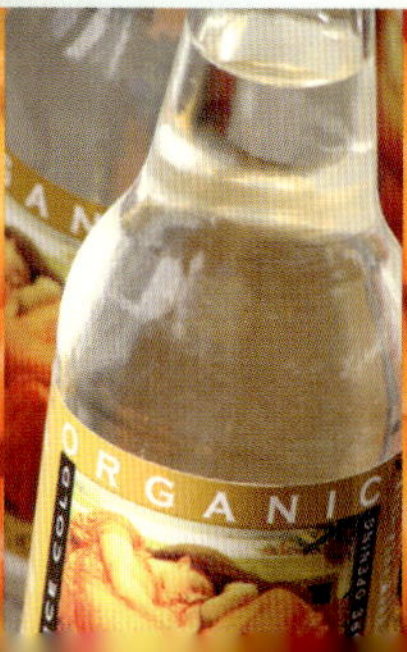
ORGANIC

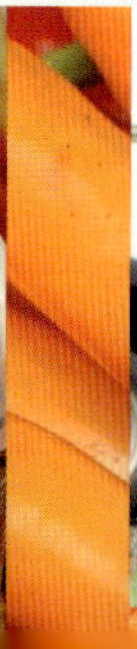

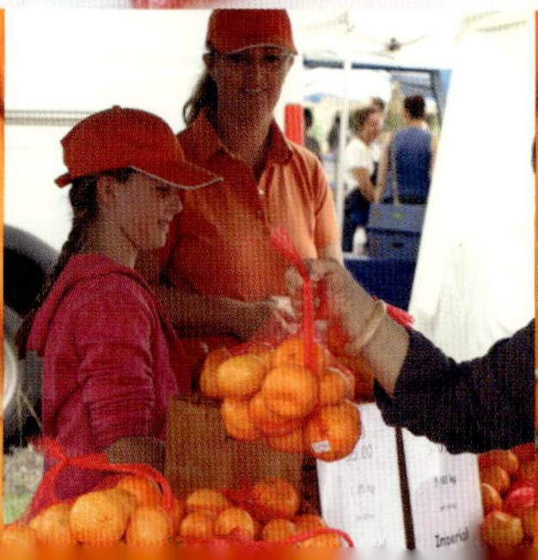

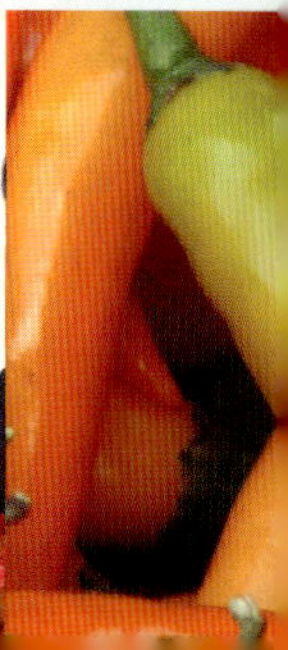

Bush Food Ravioli

Recipe by Peter Wolfe, Cedar Creek Farm

Native foods are abundant at the Noosa Farmers Markets, especially in the way of spices. Cedar Creek Farm has a wonderful selection of spices and condiments that are based on 'bush foods' and this recipe is an exciting introduction to them. You may use plain lasagne sheets although the lemon myrtle gives the dish just that little extra zest. It helps to semi-prepare the ingredients prior to beginning as you must move quite quickly once you begin cooking.

Ingredients:

12 green prawns, cutlets
6 lemon myrtle lasagne sheets
100g warrigal greens (native spinach)
1 tbs macadamia oil
12 macadamia nuts
150ml pure cream
2 spring onions, finely sliced
1 tsp ground lemon myrtle leaf
1 tsp coarsely ground mountain pepper berries
1 tsp balsamic vinegar
1 tbs lime juice
salt to taste

Method:

Peel prawns by slicing 2/3 of the way down the back to flatten out into a cutlet. Dust the prawn cutlets with the crushed mountain pepperberries and set aside. Boil lasagne sheets in lightly salted water for 12 minutes or until cooked. Blanch warrigal greens in the same water for I minute, then drain.

Heat macadamia oil in a heavy based pan and lightly brown the macadamia nuts then set aside. Quickly toss prawns in the oil until the prawns are just starting to colour. Remove from pan and place aside.

Put spring onions, cream, lemon myrtle, vinegar and lime juice in pan. Bring to a rapid boil then warm prawns in the sauce. Season with salt to taste. Turn off heat and assemble ravioli immediately.

To assemble, lay pasta sheets flat. Place one tablespoon of warrigal greens and two prawns with a small amount of the sauce on one end of the sheet. Then fold the other end over the top. When all the prawns are wrapped, arrange them on a pasta plate and top with remaining sauce. Garnish with the macadamia nuts and remaining warrigal greens.

Serves 2 as main, 3 as entrée

Sticky Lamb Shanks with Parsnip Mash

Recipe by Peter Wolfe Cedar Creek Farm

Winter brings with it the yearning for slowly cooked comfort foods and there is nothing more comforting than lamb shanks that just melt in your mouth. The combination of the honey and spice blend, add extra dimension to this dish which is complimented by the creamy parsnip mash. Try sprinkling a little finely diced preserved lemon and coriander on the shanks just prior to serving.

Ingredients:

6 lamb shanks
1 cup sherry or rice wine
2 tbs tomato sauce
1 tbs oyster sauce
1 tbs soy sauce
1 tsp English mustard
1 tsp horseradish
1 tsp turmeric powder
½ tsp five spice powder
1 tsp crushed garlic
1 tsp crushed ginger
½ cup honey
1 tbs cornflour to thicken
1 tbs water
salt & pepper to taste

Parsnip Mash:
2 large potatoes
2 large parsnips
1 tbs butter
2 tbs cream

Method:

Preheat oven to 180°C. Place lambs shanks in a baking dish. Mix together sherry/rice wine, tomato sauce, oyster sauce, soy sauce, English mustard, horseradish, turmeric, five spice powder, garlic and ginger. Pour over lamb shanks. Cover with foil and bake at 180°C until shanks are tender but not falling off the bone (approximately 2 hours), turning after about an hour. Remove from oven. Mix cornflour and water into a paste and add to the sauce until thick. Stir in the honey then place back in the oven, uncovered for a further 5 minutes on each side.

To make the mash, boil the peeled and chopped potatoes and parsnips in water. When the potatoes and parsnips are soft, drain away the water. Add cream and butter and mash together until smooth.

Serve shanks on a bed of mash with the sticky sauce coating the shanks.

Serves 6

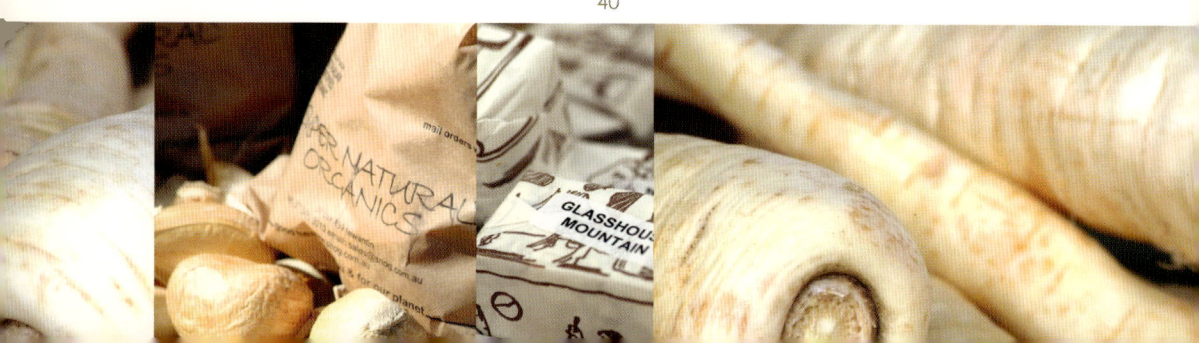

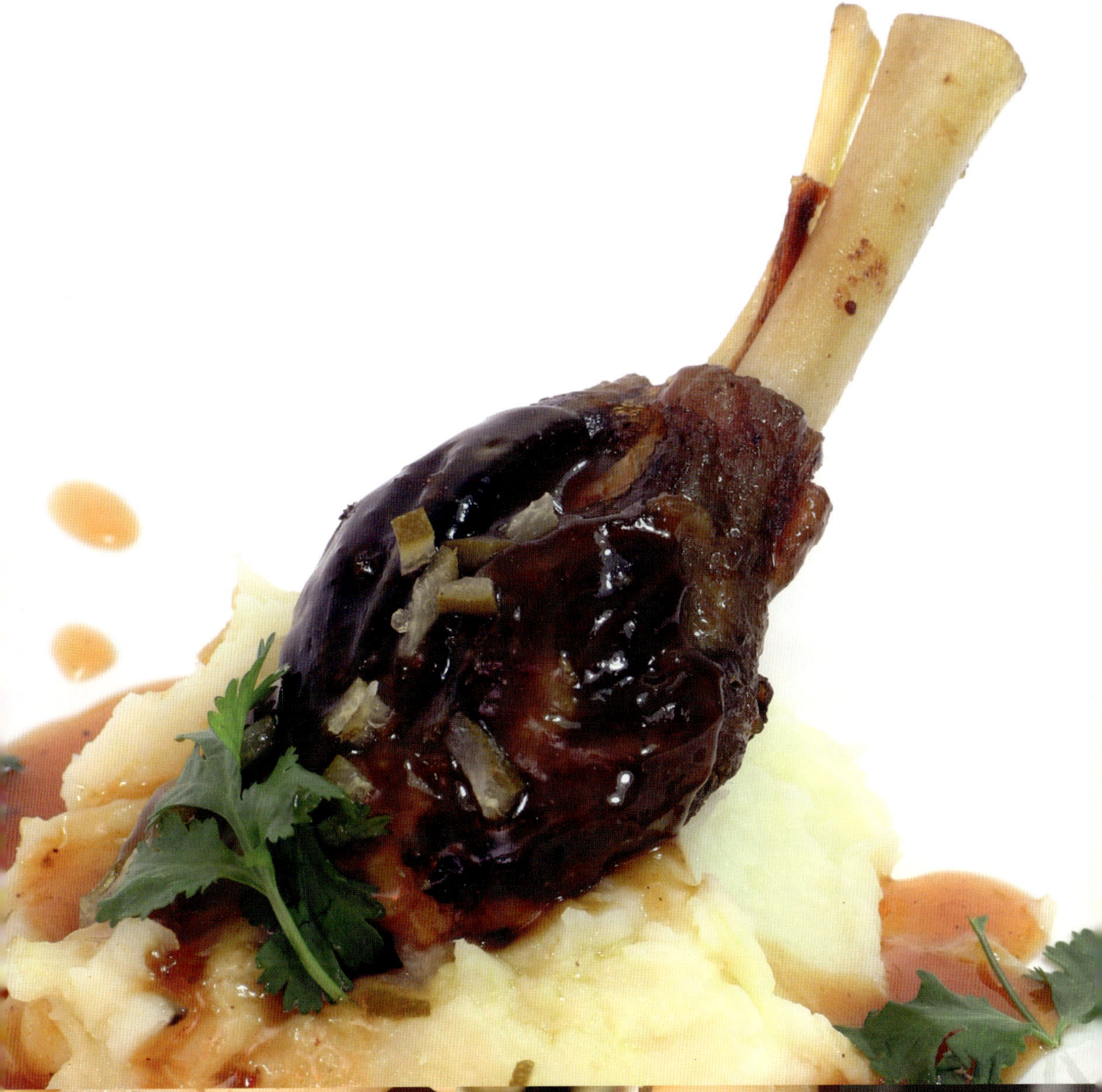
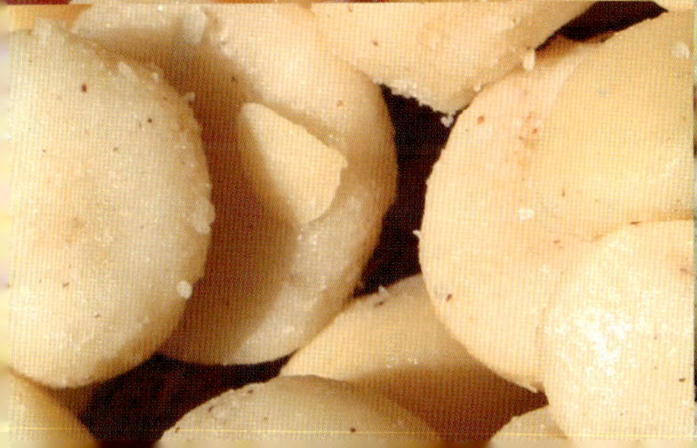
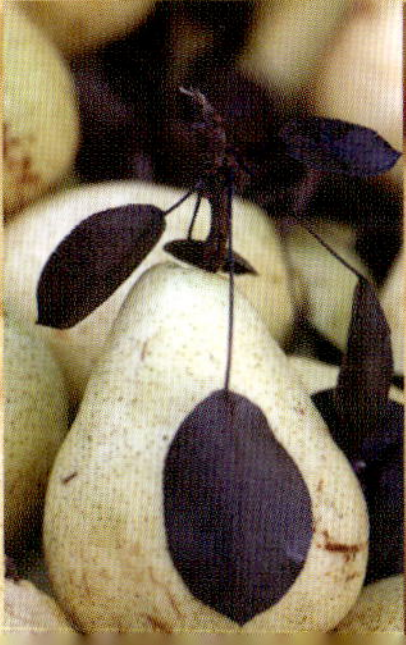
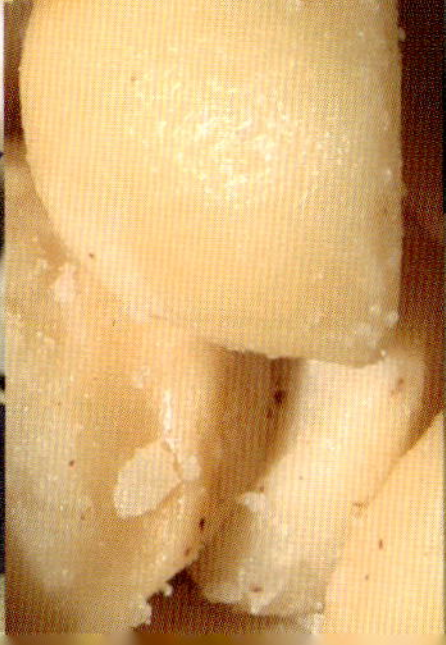
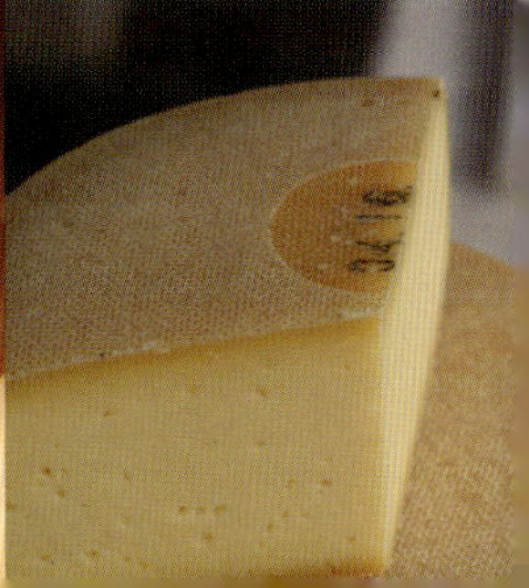

Noosa Farmers' Market Directory

A & T Produce
Boreen Pt
Free Range Eggs
Ph: 5485 0890

Aussie Gourmet Treats
Buderim
Vienna style nuts
Ph: 5444 4842

Auswana Coffee
Bracalba
locally grown coffee
Ph. 5496 4556

Back Pocket
Granite Belt
Wine
Ph. 4683 5184

Bean & Gone Coffee Cart
Sunrise Beach
hot coffee
Ph. 5448 0265 / 0421 426 053

Bedrock Herbs
Tewantin
herbs · lettuce · leafy greens
Ph. 5449 9557

Brett Blanckensee
Kandanga
watermelons · eggs · spuds
pumpkin · broccoli · cauliflower
Ph. 5484 3797

Bropar
Verridale
Bananas
Ph: 0437 826 320

Cafe Le Mundi
Cooroy
pancakes
Ph. 5449 1020 / 0402 276 930

Cedar Creek Farm
Belli Park
native foods · preserves · citrus
seasonal vegetables
Ph. 5447 0108

Chimichurri Co
Noosaville
Argentinean chimichurri sauce
Ph: 0432 598 193

Clarke Mushrooms
Woombye
swiss brown mushrooms
Ph. 5442 2140

Claude's Food
Noosa
ready made & take home salads
soups
Ph: 5441 4780 / 0422 900 875

Continental German Sausages
Eumundi
ready to eat and take home
German sausages
Ph: 5442 8586

Coolabine Goat Cheese
Kenilworth
goat's cheese
Ph. 5446 0616

Corn Connection
Noosa Waters
homemade lemonade · salad dressings
Ph. 5447 1345

Crystal Waters Bakery
Maleny
bread
Ph. 5494 4779

Dev's Herbs
Cootharaba
herbs · lettuce · tomatoes
Ph: 5485 3281 / 0421 53 00 14

Diana's Christmas Cakes & Puddings
Oakey
Christmas cakes · puddings
Ph. 4691 1422 / 0418 717 457

Doonan Fresh
Doonan
vine ripened tomatoes
Ph. 5471 0119

ECO Australia
Wolvi
locally farmed nuts
Ph. 5486 6156

EJ's Crepes
Noosaville
French Crepes and waffles
Ph: 5474 5257

Essential Grain Bakery
Noosaville
bread
Ph. 5455 6266

Eumundi Flower Lady
Eumundi
chemical free fragrant roses
Ph: 5442 7154

Eumundi Food Company
Eumundi
cakes · preserves · meringues
Christmas puddings
Ph. 0438 124 364

Eumundi Rise
Doonan
vine ripened tomatoes
Ph. 0427 358 723

Noosa Farmers' Market Directory

Eumundi Strawberries
Eumundi
strawberries
Ph. 5442 8213

Exotic Mushrooms
Bowral
exotic mushrooms
Ph. 0401 493 095

Farmer Bills
Maleny
herbs · lettuce · tomatoes
flowers · avocados
Ph: 5494 4756 / 0402 096 448

Farmer Dave
Goondiwindi
organic lamb
Ph. 0408 076 800

Fat Hen Farm
Kilkivan
olives · olive oil · dukkah
Ph. 5484 1372

Florabloom
Peachester
flowers · roses
Ph. 5494 9232

Fromart
Eudlo
semi hard Swiss style cheese
Ph. 0408 725 349

G & J Produce
Glastonbury
seasonal vegetables
Ph. 5484 0248

Gabbana's Fruit & Vegies
Kandanga
organic fruit · vegetabes
Ph. 5484 3465

Galeru
Cooroy
native rainforest berry condiments
cakes · yoghurts
Ph. 5442 5945 / 0400 439 295

German Sausage Hut
Eumundi
Take Home & ready to eat German Sausages
Ph. 0409 406 531

Golden Valley Gourmet Pies
Yandina
gourmet gluten free pies
Ph. 5446 6508 / 0413 844 623

Greek Yoghurt
Elimbah
yoghurt
Ph. 5497 4464

Gympie Cheese
Noosa Heads
cow's & goat's cheeses · yoghurts
butter
Ph. 0439 889 386

Happy Farmers
Howard
chemical free sweet potato
passionfruit drink · beauty and
health care products · free range
eggs
Ph: 4129 5697

Hello Honey
Noosa Heads
honey · honey products · jelly bush honey
Ph: 0400 196 940

Hermitage Country Crafts
Cedar Pocket
preserves · baked goods · free range eggs
Ph. 5486 6184 / 0408 279 917

Hinterland Organics
Eumundi
local organic vegetables · fruit
eggs
Ph. 0423 633 285

Hollaran's Fruit
Cottonvale
apples · stone fruit · grapes
zucchinis
Ph. 4685 2257 / 0438 506 728

Jackpot Nursery
Toogoolawah
vegie & herb seedlings
Ph: 5423 0169 / 0408 986 080

Jen Chisholm's Cakes & Puddings
Mooloolaba
Christmas cakes · puddings
Ph. 0418 733 055

John Cole
Yandina
Paw Paws
Ph. 0409 069 818

Kabi Golf Farm
Boreen Pt
organic citrus
Ph: 5485 3494

Kandara Strawberries
Morayfield
strawberries · rockmelons · mini melons · blueberries
Ph. 5497 9387

Kenilworth Organic Olive Oil
Kenilworth
organic olive oil · organic herbs
lettuce
Ph. 5447 0047

Noosa Farmers' Market Directory

Kin Kin Beef
Kin Kin
beef
Ph: 5485 4512

KH &JM McKay
Palmwoods
pineapples · ginger
Ph. 5445 0787

Lettuce Alone
Cooroy
bagged lettuce · homemade dog treats
Ph. 5442 5644

Liz's Own Anti Pasto
Greenslopes
anti pasto
Ph. 3397 9632 / 0403 38 152

LR & FJ Millard
Wolvi
oranges
Ph. 5486 7263 / 0428 867 263

Lush Plants
Caloundra
plants · orchids
Ph. 5491 1155 / 0439 791 178

Maleny Cheese
Maleny
locally crafted cheese · Maleny dairy products
Ph: 5494 2207 / 0419 913 890

Mango Shack
Woombye
mango drinks · smoothies
Ph. 5442 2674

Maple Muesli
Noosa
muesli
Ph: 1800 627 531 / 0405 361 664

Materia
Palmwoods
avocados · custard apples
Ph: 5445 0090

Mudgeeraba Spices
Mudgeeraba
Indian & Sri Lankan foods · spices
Ph. 5530 7443 / 0419 027 056

Natures Nibbles
Amamoor
seed · nut mixes
Ph. 5488 4282 / 0400 734 809

Newman's Asparagus
Nanango
asparagus · herbs
Ph. 4165 4563

Nimo's Chicken Wraps
Noosaville
Chicken Wraps
Ph: 0432 598 193

Noosa Gourmet Maccas
Sunrise Beach
local flavoured macadamias
Ph: 0447 732 757

Noosa Orchard
Lake McDonald
Avocados and Limes
Ph: 5447 6741

Noosa Reds
Noosa
vine ripened tomatoes
Ph. 5449 1668

Noosa Valley Market Garden
Doonan
small crops · lettuce · herbs
Ph. 5471 1106

North Shore Gourmet
Mudjimba
dips · jams · chutneys · pesto
Ph: 5450 7759 / 0418 153 908

Nutrifruit
Palmwoods
strawberries · avocados
Ph. 5478 9800

Pasta Riviera
Clontarf
fresh pasta · pasta sauces
Ph. 3284 2211

Plants of Palmwoods
Palmwoods
native plants · palms
Ph: 5457 3457 / 0448 281 508

Ray Atkin
Bundaberg
Vine ripened tomatoes · capsicums
Ph. 4159 3265

Slow Rise Bakery
Boreen Point
bread · cakes · biscuits
Ph. 5485 3673

Soul Food
Noosaville
New Orleans style spices · sauces foods
Ph. 0415 456 832

Spanner Crabs Noosa
Noosa Heads
spanner crabs · local seafood
Ph. 5474 8821 / 0427 766 778

Spirit of Tibet
Tibetan food
Mooloolaba
Ph: 5444 5266

Spunky Spuds
Springbrook
8 varieties of spuds
Ph. 5520 2036 / 0413 284 158

Stockman's Choice Meats
Buderim
Queensland beef · crocodile · kangaroo · gourmet meats
Ph. 5450 1031 / 0402 856 890

Sue's Organic Cuisine
Noosa
pestos and preserves
Ph. 5447 5132 / 0402 280 558

Sunray Berries
Wamuran
strawberries
Ph. 5496 7364 / 0418 732 066

Supernatural Organics
Boreen Pt
organic Australian garlic · organic seasonal fruit · vegetables asparagus
Ph: 5485 3010

Tammin
Tewantin
cut gerberas
Ph. 5473 0213 / 0427 765 132

Tasty Fruit Company
Wamuran
bananas · pineapples
Ph. 5429 8301

Tayaki
Noosa Heads
Japanese pancakes
Ph. 5474 8231

The Neem Man
Yandina
neem tree products
Ph. 0401 417 140

The Olive Guy
Caloundra
olives and anti pasto
Ph: 5491 5717

The Rolling Dolmade
Tewantin
homemade mezze
Ph. 5455 5128 / 0408 889 080

Traditions
Noosaville
hot breakfast · bacon & eggs
homemade lemonade
Ph: 0424 241 857

Uloq Mandarins
Gayndah
mandarines
Ph. 4161 1560 / 0429 611 560

Villarica
Amamoor
nectarines · passionfruit · custard apples
Ph: 5488 4371 / 0423 336 890

Waugh's Fruit & Vegetables
Gympie
fruit · vegetables
Ph. 5484 9198 / 0419 676 987

Wensley's
Southport
traditional Cornish pasties · pork pies
Ph. 5571 1806 / 0437 636 733

Wheat Grass Noosa
Noosa Heads
organic wheatgrass shots
Ph. 0407 016 095

Wild J's Blueberries
North Arm
blueberries
Ph. 5446 6010 / 0411 100 730

Wort Organics
Noosaville
organic soft drinks
Ph: 5449 8498 / 0407 643 410

Zehnder Gluten Free
Maleny
gluten free bread
Ph. 5435 2388

Acknowledgements

I have always been a great supporter of farmers' markets and the creation of this book reminded me of why. It is a special type of person that has the dedication and passion involved with growing and producing good quality food. It is one thing to do it for yourself but quite another to go through the process of sharing it with others.

I would like to thank all of the dedicated and wonderful people at the Noosa Farmers' Market for bringing us fresh, vibrant and often quite innovative, healthy and wholesome food. Thank you to these same people for their assistance in the creation of this book; the smiles, the chats, the colourful stalls that have provided great inspiration in the photographing of the book and of course the wonderful food that I so frequently enjoy. If there is anyone that I have overlooked by way of inclusion in this book, I apologise; it has not been intentional, merely an oversight and by no means should be interpreted as a reflection of their product or commitment to the markets.

A special thanks for the delicious recipes that have been generously provided by:
Matt Golinski (The Rolling Dolmade - www.therollingdolmade.com.au) **Peter Wolfe** (Cedar Creek Farm - www.localharvest.com.au/content/view/84/118) **Mary Bowtle** (The Eumundi Food Company) **Brent Southcombe** (Designed 2 Taste - www.designed2taste.com.au) Thank you also to **Maggie Ensor** (Gypsy Photographics) for some of the wonderful photography featuring the market stalls and stall holders on pages 8,9,24 and 25.

The biggest thanks of all goes to **Shane Stanley**, firstly for having the vision to begin the farmers' market in the first place, second for his ongoing commitment to regional food and the markets and thirdly for his help and assistance throughout the creation of this book.

Thanks to my family and friends for their ongoing encouragement and support, my partner Don especially, who patiently takes a back seat while I constantly traipse off to markets or work until late in the night to complete the projects I undertake.

And last but not least, thank you to all the people that support the Farmers' Market through purchasing produce or by way of spreading the word as you are just as important to the sustainability of these fabulous regional industries as the growers and producers and together we can all do our bit to preserve the quality and integrity of our food.

Noosa Farmers' Markets

For stall directory and general information see:
www.noosafarmersmarket.com.au

Every Sunday morning until noon
Aussie Rules Football Grounds
Weyba Road
Noosaville, Sunshine Coast, Queensland
Ph. 0418 769 374

Useful Websites

For information about Sunshine Coast Growers and Producers see:
www.localharvest.com.au

For Sunshine Coast Regional Food Initiatives see:
www.regionalfoodie.com.au